SHURLEY ENGLISH

Level 7

Practice Booklet
For Introductory & Practice Sentences

SHURLEY INSTRUCTIONAL MATERIALS, INC., CABOT, ARKANSAS

11-19
ISBN-13: 978-1-58561-097-6
ISBN-10: 1-58561-097-6
(Level 7 Practice Booklet)

Printed in the United States of America by LSC Communications, Owensville, MO.

For additional information or to place an order, write to: Shurley Instructional Materials, Inc.
366 SIM Drive
Cabot, AR 72023

1 2 3 4 5 6 7 19 17 15 12 09 07 04

CHAPTER 2 INTRODUCTORY SENTENCES FOR LESSON 1

1. Doctor spoke.
2. Horses ran.
3. Speaker arrived.
4. Monkey chattered.
5. A brilliant doctor spoke reluctantly.
6. Several chestnut horses ran fast.
7. The keynote speaker arrived late yesterday.
8. The small tropical monkey chattered noisily.
9. ____________ A brilliant doctor spoke reluctantly.
10. ____________ Several chestnut horses ran fast.
11. ____________ The keynote speaker arrived late yesterday.
12. ____________ The small tropical monkey chattered noisily.

CHAPTER 2 PRACTICE SENTENCES FOR LESSON 2

1. ____________ An extremely brilliant doctor spoke very reluctantly.
2. ____________ Several chestnut horses ran surprisingly fast.
3. ____________ The famous keynote speaker arrived extremely late.
4. ____________ Those two small tropical monkeys chattered quite noisily.
5. ____________ A very hungry alligator lurked dangerously below.

CHAPTER 3 INTRODUCTORY SENTENCES FOR LESSON 1

1. ____________ The floppy-eared spaniel howled mournfully in the dark house.

2. ____________ The intense runners anxiously raced forward at the sound of the gun.

3. ____________ After summer vacation the football players eagerly gathered around the coach in the locker room.

4. ____________ Yesterday the dense fog finally lifted in the late afternoon.

5. ____________ Today the band members worked very hard on the competition music.

CHAPTER 3 PRACTICE SENTENCES FOR LESSON 2

1. ____________ During a heavy snowstorm the daring skier raced for help for the stranded family.

2. ____________ Several yellow helium balloons rose gracefully to the ceiling.

3. ____________ The long line of camels plodded steadily across the hot desert.

4. ____________ The scientific instrument flashed at a dangerously low level on the monitor.

5. ____________ The two nighthawks usually feed heavily after a rainstorm.

CHAPTER 4 INTRODUCTORY SENTENCES FOR LESSON 1

1. ____________ He slept on a crude bed of pine boughs in the cold cave.

2. ____________ Wait patiently for the mail.

3. ____________ Two cold, tired skiers stood in front of me in the long line for the ski lift in Colorado.

4. ____________ In the late afternoon the boys in the street yelled at us for a ride to the basketball game.

5. ____________ Run to the window for a closer look at the President!

CHAPTER 4 PRACTICE SENTENCES FOR LESSON 2

1. ____________ She stopped on the treacherous trail for a brief rest during the long journey.

2. ____________ Watch for the robins at the feeder in the early morning.

3. ____________ A large flock of geese suddenly swooped into the corn fields.

4. ____________ They gasped in disbelief at the stunning view below them!

5. ____________ Clean thoroughly under the refrigerator in the kitchen.

CHAPTER 5 INTRODUCTORY SENTENCES FOR LESSON 1

1. ___________ My sister talked patiently to her little kitten.

2. ___________ Run to Grandma's house after supper.

3. ___________ During the blizzard the wolf's cubs impatiently waited in the shelter of the trees for their mother.

4. ___________ A family of congenial bears lived in their spacious cave at the edge of a magnificent forest.

5. ___________ For several hours he worked steadily on his brother's motorcycle.

CHAPTER 5 PRACTICE SENTENCES FOR LESSON 2

1. ___________ He limped painfully into the doctor's office.

2. ___________ The diamond on her finger sparkled in its simple setting.

3. ___________ For three days we floated on a small raft in the middle of the huge ocean.

4. ___________ Go to Mrs. Conway's desk for your homework assignment in math.

5. ___________ Our town's oldest house is on the old river road.

CHAPTER 6 INTRODUCTORY SENTENCES FOR LESSON 1

1. ____________ The five little beagle pups were barking impatiently for their mother's return.

2. ____________ I did not walk carefully down the slippery steps on my way to school.

3. ____________ Were those antique chairs sold at the auction yesterday?

4. ____________ Did Cinderella ride to the ball in an orange pumpkin coach?

5. ____________ The stolen items from Colonel Glen's house were never found by the police.

CHAPTER 6 PRACTICE SENTENCES FOR LESSON 2

1. ____________ The frightened kitten was carried from the tall tree by our sympathetic neighbor.

2. ____________ The temperature of the water at the fish hatchery has never varied over a few degrees.

3. ____________ Are you preparing for a very long trip to Alaska?

4. ____________ The water for our oatmeal is boiling briskly in the pot on the stove.

5. ____________ The mountain lion was creeping slowly toward the children!

CHAPTER 7 INTRODUCTORY SENTENCES FOR LESSON 1

1. ____________ The men and women walked quietly in single file.

2. ____________ Dogsleds and huskies are not used for transportation by the majority of the people in Alaska.

3. ____________ The soldiers crawled through the fields and ran for their lives under enemy fire.

4. ____________ Wow! The race car crashed into the wall at a tremendous speed!

5. ____________ Whew! The mountain climbers gasped and panted in the thin air yesterday.

CHAPTER 7 PRACTICE SENTENCES FOR LESSON 2

1. ____________ A scrawny cow and her calf stood under the oak tree during the storm.

2. ____________ A group of wet and hungry boys huddled around the small campfire.

3. ____________ Incredible! A fight erupted in the stands after the soccer game!

4. ____________ My father's overalls and farm shirt are hanging behind the barn door.

5. ____________ The old farmer and his wife had never gone outside their little township.

CHAPTER 8 INTRODUCTORY SENTENCES FOR LESSON 1

1. ____________ In California thousands of tourists camp in Yosemite National Park annually.

2. ____________ Has the original gold field or the main diamond bed in Canada been found?

3. ____________ An extremely bashful little girl in a pink dress tearfully searched for her mother in the crowded store.

4. ____________ Wait patiently for your father's arrival.

5. ____________ Help! That farmer's corn fields are burning!

CHAPTER 8 PRACTICE SENTENCES FOR LESSON 2

1. ____________ Frank and Jeff can drive around the practice course after business hours.

2. ____________ Sam and his family hike for miles in the woods behind their house.

3. ____________ Oh yes! The little girls at the surprise birthday party giggled constantly!

4. ____________ Yesterday we laughed and clapped hysterically at the antics of the funny clowns.

5. ____________ My brother talked patiently with an indignant customer for an hour yesterday.

CHAPTER 9 INTRODUCTORY SENTENCES FOR LESSON 1

1. ____________ Has my father's shipment of strawberries been delivered to our warehouse?
2. ____________ The strawberry pie on the table was gone quickly.
3. ____________ My sister's family did not go to Hawaii or Alaska for their summer vacation.
4. ____________ My uncle's magnificent stallion wheeled and pranced proudly to the far end of the corral!
5. ____________ My parents live in a quaint little house on the side of the mountain in the hills of Kentucky.

CHAPTER 9 PRACTICE SENTENCES FOR LESSON 2

1. ____________ My little brother's toys were piled in the middle of the floor in his bedroom.
2. ____________ On weekends my mother and father walk rapidly around the lake before breakfast.
3. ____________ Janet or Toni is going to the party at Grant's house on Saturday.
4. ____________ Many fans have come to the game without their umbrellas.
5. ____________ Were those antique vases sold at the auction early yesterday?

CHAPTER 10 INTRODUCTORY SENTENCES FOR LESSON 1

1. __________ David and Sherry painted the mural in the hall.

2. __________ The camera operator moved the camera to different positions.

3. __________ Did your brother study architecture in college?

4. __________ The famous journalist will write news stories about the war.

5. __________ California's valleys always require irrigation for their crops.

CHAPTER 10 PRACTICE SENTENCES FOR LESSON 2

1. __________ Joe easily pried the lids off the two glass jars on the kitchen table.

2. __________ The weasel suddenly struck and firmly clutched the frightened squirrel.

3. __________ My friend won a cash award for her poetry.

4. __________ We finally located a motel and a restaurant in a small town in eastern Nebraska.

5. __________ Did the principal suspend him?

CHAPTER 11 INTRODUCTORY SENTENCES FOR LESSON 1

1. ____________ The big family of brown rabbits finally located a safe site for their new home.

2. ____________ The Indians of the Northwest designed and carved totem poles in their villages.

3. ____________ Always secure your carry-on luggage during a rough jet flight.

4. ____________ My aunt did not recognize us in our Halloween costumes.

5. ____________ Wow! The police spotted the thief behind the hedges across the street!

CHAPTER 11 PRACTICE SENTENCES FOR LESSON 2

1. ____________ Amazing! A toad can grab and eat an insect in seconds!

2. ____________ My dad took his first trip to Disneyworld at the age of sixty-two.

3. ____________ The pilot of an airplane always inspects his plane thoroughly before take-off.

4. ____________ They had included a set of important safety instructions with the purchase of the appliance.

5. ____________ He ordered a delicious dessert with chocolate sprinkles.

CHAPTER 12 INTRODUCTORY SENTENCES FOR LESSON 1

1. ____________ During study time Toby never raises his eyes from the material before him.

2. ____________ Lynn and Sara gave their demonstrations without any practice.

3. ____________ The young hunters gazed eagerly at the deer in the meadow.

4. ____________ Lumberjacks at work will sometimes sing songs with strong rhythm.

5. ____________ The patient had walked away from the hospital during the night!

CHAPTER 12 PRACTICE SENTENCES FOR LESSON 2

1. ____________ The dentist's stool rolled swiftly across the floor and bumped into the wall.

2. ____________ I did not take many detailed notes during the legislative session.

3. ____________ Did the coach inspire and encourage his team before the big game?

4. ____________ Yikes! Look at that enormous snake behind the door!

5. ____________ Put the meat and vegetables on the table for dinner.

CHAPTER 13 INTRODUCTORY SENTENCES FOR LESSON 1

1. ____________ My best friend sent me a secret message.

2. ____________ The famous writer showed me the first draft of his new book.

3. ____________ My sister's friends in Alaska gave her a scrapbook with beautiful photographs of their beloved frozen tundra.

4. ____________ My dad built Tommy a treehouse for his birthday.

5. ____________ The restaurant gave me a uniform for my waitress job.

CHAPTER 13 PRACTICE SENTENCES FOR LESSON 2

1. ____________ Give the policeman your license and registration papers during a routine stop.

2. ____________ Sam and Joe baked me a surprise birthday cake.

3. ____________ He will surely show us his new tennis racket.

4. ____________ The children drew their teacher a highly-detailed picture of their playground.

5. ____________ Did our English teacher give us a special assignment for second semester?

CHAPTER 14 INTRODUCTORY SENTENCES FOR LESSON 1

1. ____________ The two brothers and their friends sold everyone lemonade from their lemonade stand on the corner of their street during July and August.

2. ____________ Our father gave us good advice during our teen years.

3. ____________ Yesterday the owners of the hotel sent my uncle's company a big bill for the convention ball.

4. ____________ My sister's husband generously sent her a dozen yellow roses for her birthday.

5. ____________ After the game the fans gave the football players a loud round of applause.

CHAPTER 14 PRACTICE SENTENCES FOR LESSON 2

1. ____________ Don gave Coach Adams the message before the game.

2. ____________ Grandma served Linda and me cookies and milk for our snack after school.

3. ____________ At the crowded theater the usher finally found Billy and Mary seats together.

4. ____________ We gleefully bought our pet a new leash with flashing lights!

5. ____________ Will you send me your new address in Florida?

CHAPTER 15 INTRODUCTORY SENTENCES FOR LESSON 1

1. ____________ Did James and John look for the others at their sister's wedding reception?

2. ____________ The basketball fans rode the school bus to the state basketball finals.

3. ____________ I wanted peach cobbler with ice cream for dessert.

4. ____________ Teach Johnny and me a few basic rules about fishing for bass.

5. ____________ Our new neighbors generously offered us their cottage on the lake for two weeks!

CHAPTER 15 PRACTICE SENTENCES FOR LESSON 2

1. ____________ Will you make us blueberry pancakes for breakfast tomorrow?

2. ____________ Many serious-minded students in American, English, and French schools have held worthwhile discussions on the importance of critical thinking.

3. ____________ Write the title and author of your book on a title page for your report.

4. ____________ The little old lady in the yellow hat gave the owner of the store a lecture on manners and responsibility.

5. ____________ My friends and I went to the game and cheered loudly for our team.

CHAPTER 16 INTRODUCTORY SENTENCES FOR LESSON 1

1. ____________ Many early settlers were farmers.

2. ____________ Florida's main crop is oranges.

3. ____________ His first newspaper assignment was an investigation of a public official in New York City.

4. ____________ The attractive girl in the yellow dress and shoes is she.

5. ____________ My favorite uncle became a successful journalist in the newspaper business.

CHAPTER 16 PRACTICE SENTENCES FOR LESSON 2

1. ____________ The Grand Canyon is the largest gorge in the world!

2. ____________ The best players on the team are you and Joey.

3. ____________ The tuba and trumpet are favorite brass instruments for many musicians.

4. ____________ A thesaurus is a book of synonyms and antonyms.

5. ____________ Flour and milk are the main ingredients for this delicious recipe.

CHAPTER 17 INTRODUCTORY SENTENCES FOR LESSON 1

1. ____________ The musician was a professional player of the violin and piano.

2. ____________ The Kentucky Derby is the most famous race for horses in this country.

3. ____________ Science and math are my most challenging subjects.

4. ____________ The human mind is an incredibly complicated instrument.

5. ____________ The winner of the first race was he.

CHAPTER 17 PRACTICE SENTENCES FOR LESSON 2

1. ____________ The business before the committee is the dance in March for the benefit of the drama department.

2. ____________ My brother's first three gifts were basketballs.

3. ____________ Amethyst is another name for purple quartz.

4. ____________ Mary Ann was secretary of her class during her senior year.

5. ____________ Mount Vernon is the former home and burial place of George Washington.

CHAPTER 18 INTRODUCTORY SENTENCES FOR LESSON 1

1. ____________ The undercover agent cleverly short-circuited the electrical system.
2. ____________ My mother and father in Mexico sent me some Mexican money.
3. ____________ The rescue workers with food and medical supplies arrived in helicopters at the isolated village on the frozen prairie.
4. ____________ The barracuda is a dangerous fish.
5. ____________ The excessive heat and high humidity in July caused almost unbearable discomfort.

CHAPTER 18 PRACTICE SENTENCES FOR LESSON 2

1. ____________ After the steep climb the tired and thirsty hikers stopped at a roadside stand for lemonade and hamburgers.
2. ____________ Greedy King Midas turned objects into shiny gold in his huge palace.
3. ____________ The horses rapidly raced to the barn during the electrical storm.
4. ____________ Mr. Smith sold them three boxes of stationery.
5. ____________ My favorite little car is the Volkswagen.

CHAPTER 19 INTRODUCTORY SENTENCES FOR LESSON 1

1. ____________ The downhill skier looked nervous before the state competition.

2. ____________ The microwave oven on display is very expensive.

3. ____________ This potato soup tastes delicious!

4. ____________ The voters in this city are leery of the current solutions to major problems.

5. ____________ Our dinner portions at the banquet were quite modest.

CHAPTER 19 PRACTICE SENTENCES FOR LESSON 2

1. ____________ My favorite suit was quite expensive.

2. ____________ The rocks and crevices were tough on the climbers.

3. ____________ The brothers' journey was terribly difficult.

4. ____________ The young football players were very strong for their age.

5. ____________ Henry has been ill for two days.

CHAPTER 20 INTRODUCTORY SENTENCES FOR LESSON 1

1. ____________ The restaurant food is Italian and delicious!
2. ____________ The Hawaiian climate is unusually delightful during spring, summer, autumn, or winter.
3. ____________ The blossoming peach orchards appear entirely pink.
4. ____________ The little village in the Alps has grown quite large.
5. ____________ He looks very handsome in that picture.

CHAPTER 20 PRACTICE SENTENCES FOR LESSON 2

1. ____________ The strange cat looked hungry and thin.
2. ____________ These math problems are very easy for me.
3. ____________ Those new shoes are too tight on my sister's feet.
4. ____________ The long voyage has been boring and dull.
5. ____________ Some girls' hairstyles are cute.

CHAPTER 21 INTRODUCTORY SENTENCES FOR LESSON 1

1. ____________ That perfume smells too strong for me!

2. ____________ Did Sam wear his new Austrian hat to the meeting?

3. ____________ The brave captain shouted angrily at the mutinous crew.

4. ____________ Those are outrageous costumes for the party!

5. ____________ Show us your new tennis racket.

CHAPTER 21 PRACTICE SENTENCES FOR LESSON 2

1. ____________ His two shiny pistols look very dangerous.

2. ____________ This is our favorite movie.

3. ____________ One of our friends buys and repairs old furniture.

4. ____________ Everybody in both clubs is invited to the big celebration tonight.

5. ____________ None of the soldiers gave the enemy colonel information about their secret mission.

CHAPTER 22 INTRODUCTORY SENTENCES FOR LESSON 1

1. ____________ The President appointed him general.
2. ____________ President Abe Lincoln appointed Ulysses S. Grant general of the Union army.
3. ____________ We thought it a wonderful view!
4. ____________ Jed painted the barn red.
5. ____________ That new movie made him successful.
6. ____________ The powdered dye colored that white shirt in the sink pale blue.

CHAPTER 22 PRACTICE SENTENCES FOR LESSON 2

1. ____________ The king declared the court jester worthy of noble knighthood.
2. ____________ They considered the new student brilliant.
3. ____________ In our small town the citizens chose David "Man of the Year."
4. ____________ The elderly lady thought the young boy helpful.
5. ____________ Everyone considered him a giant in the business world.
6. ____________ Did the genie in the movie make Aladdin successful?

CHAPTER 23 INTRODUCTORY SENTENCES FOR LESSON 1

1. ___________ The president of our company appointed Diane sales director.

2. ___________ We considered the view breathtaking!

3. ___________ We consider Mr. Smith the best teacher in our science department.

4. ___________ The members of the club have elected Casey president.

CHAPTER 23 PRACTICE SENTENCES FOR LESSON 2

1. ___________ The coach calls this team his best one.

2. ___________ The majority of the men considered daily jogging very healthy.

3. ___________ They thought us complete idiots at the beginning of the project.

4. ___________ The policeman thought the elephant a traffic hazard.